THE GREAT HERO

the Great Hero

St. Paul the Apostle

WRITTEN AND ILLUSTRATED

BY THE DAUGHTERS OF ST. PAUL

ST. PAUL EDITIONS

NIHIL OBSTAT:

Rt. Rev. Matthew P. Stapleton
Diocesan Censor

IMPRIMATUR:

✝ Richard Cardinal Cushing

Library of Congress Catalog Card Number: 63-15968

Copyright,   by the *Daughters of St. Paul*

Printed in U.S.A. by the *Daughters of St. Paul*
50 St. Paul's Ave., Jamaica Plain, Boston 30, Mass.

CONTENTS

9

INTRODUCTION

Would you like to hear a story about a hero? The man we are speaking of is not a famous baseball player, or a champion swimmer, or a football star. No! He is greater than any of these men. He is not a hero of sports, but a hero of Christ! He is St. Paul the Apostle, who in his time won more souls for Christ than any other apostle of all times.

Adventure-packed was Paul's life—full of long journeys, clever escapes, shipwrecks, imprisonments, mysterious persons, wicked governors, princes and judges. Few men have faced the odds Paul faced. Fewer still have stood up to them with such strength and bravery.

In the words of Paul himself, he suffered, "in many more labors, in prisons more frequently, in lashes above measure, often exposed to death. From the Jews five times I received forty lashes less one. Thrice I was scourged, once I was stoned, thrice I suffered shipwreck, a night and a day I was adrift on the sea; in journeyings often, in perils from floods, in perils from robbers, in perils from my own nation, in perils from the Gentiles, in perils in the city, in perils in the wilderness, in perils in the sea, in perils from false brethren; in labor and hardships, in many sleepless nights, in hunger and thirst, in fastings often, in cold and nakedness. Besides those outer things, there is my daily pressing anxiety, the care of all the churches!"

Here is his story—the story of a courageous fighter, a daring apostle and a great lover of Christ and of men!

1

Saul Grows
to Manhood

Almost two thousand years ago during the time of Jesus, the Romans ruled the whole world. One famous city of this Roman Empire was Tarsus in Asia Minor. In this city lived a rich Hebrew couple. They were the father and mother of a little baby whom they named Saul in honor of the first Hebrew King, Saul.

At the age of five this little boy began to study the Holy Bible. In school, Saul showed himself to be very smart and brimful of energy.

He was a loving son, too, and felt great sorrow when his mother lay dying.

"Mama, you cannot die," he cried. "Then I will be all alone."

"No, my son," his mother whispered bravely. "You will not be alone. Your father and your dear sister will be with you."

Saul's father was very rich. Still, the boy had to learn a trade in order to support himself while studying to become a doctor of the Jewish Law. Like his father, Saul learned the craft of tentmaking and was a very hard worker, too.

How glad Saul was that his home city stood on the banks of the river, Cydnus. High-spirited and adventurous, he enjoyed running with his playmates along the docks to see the huge ships tied up there. "Look!" Saul would cry to his companions. "This is a Roman ship! And those merchants over there are also Romans. Listen to them speak Latin!"

"That ship came from Greece!" one of his friends would exclaim, pointing to another big boat. So the young boys happily scrambled back and forth on the piers, each shouting to the others over some new wonder he had discovered.

Saul also loved sports. He enjoyed watching the foot races, javelin-throwing contests, and wrestling matches held in Tarsus.

As all good Hebrews of his time, Saul longed for the coming of the Savior, promised by God to the Hebrew people. When he prayed, the lad turned toward Jerusalem and repeated the words of the famous Hebrew prophets: "Come, O Lord, our Savior, and do not delay!" Saul did not know that the promised Savior had already come and was living in Nazareth, a tiny town in the hill country of Palestine. The Savior had not yet shown Himself for what He truly was. He was living a hidden life as a humble carpenter.

When Saul reached his twelfth birthday, his father sent him to Jerusalem to study the laws of the Hebrew religion under the best Hebrew teachers called Rabbis. How excited he was the day he left Tarsus for Jerusalem! This great city was not full of idols as were many other cities. No! In Jerusalem stood the glorious Hebrew Temple, where Hebrews worshipped the true God. At this time the high priest in Jerusalem was Caiphas and the Roman ruler of the city was Pontius Pilate, who governed from the Tower of Antonia.

When Saul reached Jerusalem, he and his father went to his sister's house. He planned to live with her while he studied in this great city.

At the school of the famous Rabbi, Gamaliel, Saul and another boy, Stephen, showed themselves to be the smartest and most eager students. Often the two young Hebrew boys had completely opposite ideas.

One day they were arguing over what the promised Savior would be like. "He will be a great king!" declared Saul. "The prophet Daniel says that he shall be given glory and a kingdom and that all peoples and nations shall serve Him. He will be the strongest king on earth and will punish anyone who goes against our religion."

"No," protested Stephen, "He will be humble in whatever He does. The prophet Isaias wrote, 'He shall not cry, nor lift up, nor cause his voice to be heard in the street.' Ezechiel also tells us that he will be merciful and forgiving and that he will make all the sick people well."

Saul rapidly grew to manhood. People threw admiring glances at the slender, black-haired youth as he strode boldly through the crowded streets of Jerusalem. Eagerness and fire burned in Saul's dark eyes. His strong will showed forth in the firm set of his jaw. Saul's tan face wore an expression of self-confidence and of pride—pride in his nation, in his people who alone worshipped the one, true God!

Young Saul and his sister often attended the social gatherings of the best families in Jerusalem. Even though his friends had fun at these parties, Saul did not care for them at all.

Many of his fellow students were getting married and they were all wondering what young woman Saul would choose for his wife. "Saul," one of his companions asked him one day, "When are you going to get married?"

"Never," declared Saul firmly. "I want to dedicate myself entirely to the glory of our great Hebrew nation."

While other young men took pleasure in fine clothes, shining weapons and beautiful horses, Saul delighted in only one thing—the Bible. He would sit cross-legged for hours reading and rereading his parchment scrolls of this great book. He memorized the words of the Bible by heart—in both Greek and Hebrew.

This unusual behavior disturbed Saul's sister. "Saul," she once told him while leaning over his shoulder, "you look so tired. I am worried about you."

17

"There is no need to worry about me," Saul answered gently, as he adjusted the oil lamp hanging above his head. "You know how I am. When a great idea burns within me, I cannot rest."

Several months later Saul finished his studies of the Bible and prepared to return to Tarsus. Rather sorrowfully he took leave of each of his friends. What good times they had had together—exploring the narrow streets and hidden ways of Jerusalem, attending the public races and wrestling matches and especially listening to the explanation of the Bible given by Gamaliel.

"When will we see each other again, Stephen?" Saul asked as he gripped his fellow student's hand in a warm handshake.

"Let us hope we will meet again in happy days of love, goodness, and peace, which are about to come," Stephen replied.

✿　✿　✿

Several years passed. Jesus of Nazareth presented Himself as the promised Savior. "My teaching is not my own," Jesus preached to the crowds in the Temple, "but is from Him, Who sent Me."

* * *

Saul, now in Tarsus, heard stories of what Jesus had said and hated Him immediately. "This Jesus is an enemy of our religion!" Saul told his father angrily as the two of them were eating their evening meal.

"Now, Saul, you cannot believe everything you hear," his father replied calmly.

"But it is true, Father," the young man insisted fiercely. "Old Baruch, the wine merchant, saw and heard this man preaching the last time he went to Jerusalem! People should not listen to this faker! When I go back to Jerusalem I will punish these followers of His!"

2

The Young Persecutor

Meanwhile Jesus ended His mission on earth by dying on the cross. One of His last acts was one of love and mercy as He forgave the good thief and promised him, "This day you will be with Me in paradise."

❈   ❈   ❈

Very soon afterwards Saul returned to Jerusalem. On his first day in that city he met his old friend Stephen in the market place. Joyfully Saul greeted him, "Stephen, my friend! It is a pleasure to see you! How have you been?"

"Saul!" exclaimed the other youth. "Peace be to you, my brother!"

The two young Hebrews then moved aside to make way for a herd of goats being driven by a stout farmer into the center of the square. Quickly the young men strode to a quieter corner of the busy market place and began to talk of the latest happenings in Jerusalem.

Stephen immediately told Saul of the promised Savior Who had come to the city. But as soon as Saul realized that this Savior was none other than the Jesus of Nazareth who had been crucified, he burst out angrily, "Be quiet! How dare you speak of this faker as the promised Savior!"

"But the many miracles He worked prove His teachings to be true," argued Stephen, ignoring Saul's threatening fist. "He fulfills perfectly all the Bible's prophecies about the Savior, and best of all He has risen from the dead!"

"From now on, we are enemies!" declared Saul in fury. His eyes snapped with anger. "Anyone who believes in this Jesus cannot be my friend! And you have not heard the last of this, either!" Then giving Stephen a furious look, Saul turned on his heel and rushed down a dark, narrow side street.

Despite Saul's threat, Stephen continued to speak of his beloved Master to all who would listen. The wonders and conversions that he worked stirred up the jealousy of many of the religious authorities. One day as Stephen was preaching on the steps of the great Jewish Temple, a group of his enemies took him prisoner and marched him into the great council hall before the high priests. Stephen defended himself calmly, "What I say is the truth! You refuse to believe me because you will not permit the grace of God to come into your souls."

The crowd that filled the council hall, and Saul with them, became furious at Stephen's words. "Traitor! Liar!" they cried. Stephen knew they were wild with anger, but he would not take back what he had said about Jesus.

With a roar of loud voices and the thunder of running feet, the men rushed at Stephen. Saul was the wildest among them. They knocked Stephen down and dragged him out of the council hall.

They pulled him through the Temple and along the streets until they reached a hole they had dug. Into this they threw him. Saul, mad with fury, leaped upon a heap of stones and shouted at the crowd, "Kill him! Kill the traitor!"

"Hold my cloak, Saul," cried one of the men, throwing the garment at Saul's feet.

"And mine, too," cried another, "so I can throw the stones better!"

In the middle of this hail storm of rocks lay Stephen, dirty and bleeding, but with an expression of deep peace upon his face. Turning his eyes toward heaven, he whispered hoarsely his last prayer, "Lord Jesus, do not hold this sin against them!"

Hours later, Saul returned alone to the rocky spot where Stephen had died. By this time the other Christians had carried away the dead youth's body for proper burial. A few torn pieces of Stephen's clothing hung upon the the sharp stones scattered about on the ground. The sun stained the sky blood-red as it sank behind the high, black city walls.

No sound could be heard except the distant noises of the city. But there was no silence in Saul's heart. As he glared sullenly upon the muddy, rocky ground, a storm of anger roared inside of him. Just to kill one Christian was not enough! He clenched his fists tightly and pounded them together. All the Christians must die! He would see to it! "I will never rest," he promised himself, "until every Christian is dead!"

3

On the Road to Damascus

From that day on, Saul became the most furious persecutor of the Christians. With his band of cut-throats, he searched the cities and villages of Palestine to find them. He arrested without mercy every Christian he found. "Curse the crucifix or you will die!" he threatened them.

So terrible a persecutor was Saul that his very name filled the Christians with dread. In terror they fled from Palestine. But Saul was not a man of half measures. Going to Caiphas, the high priest, he asked for official permission to search out and arrest Christians everywhere. "I must begin at once!" he told Caiphas, when the high priest granted him permission to do so.

The very next morning, Saul and his companions headed for the city of Damascus. "Forward!" he shouted to the others, as he dug his spurs into his horse's side. "Death to the Christians!" Galloping swiftly along, Saul felt proud of himself. He had planned this new attack upon the Christians so well. He had foreseen everything, except the unexpected. . . .

Suddenly blue-black clouds filled the sky, blotting out the bright sunshine. A mysterious wind ruffled the riders' cloaks. The other men began to slow their horses down, but not Saul.

"Looks like a storm is coming up," one of the riders remarked.

"Wait, Saul!" another man shouted. "Slow down! Wait for us!"

"Not me!" Saul called back, spurring his horse on to even greater speed. Crouching low over his swiftly moving mount, the daring young leader refused to be slowed down by the thunder or the darkness of the storm. Nothing would stop him!

Suddenly a streak of lightning flashed before Saul's eyes. In terror, his horse reared. Astonished, Saul clung to the reins with all his might. Fear flooded his heart as he felt himself knocked off his horse by a mysterious power. Lying in a crumpled heap on the rocky road, Saul saw before him a glorious figure. Standing straight and tall, this mysterious person looked at Saul sadly and seriously. "Saul, Saul," He asked gently, "why do you persecute Me?"

Frightened and shaken, Saul could only gasp hoarsely, "Who are you, Lord?"

"I am Jesus of Nazareth, Whom you persecute," came the answer.

In that instant Saul understood everything clearly. Jesus of Nazareth was the promised Savior, the Son of God! Generous and upright, Saul only wanted to do God's will. Now that he saw that Jesus was God, he wanted to obey Him completely. With all his heart and soul, he was won over to Jesus. Now he would follow Him with unfailing love and courage for the rest of his life! Humbly, Saul whispered his surrender to his Lord and his God, "Lord, what will you have me do?"

"Arise and go into the city, and you will be told what to do," Jesus told him and then vanished.

Hurled from his horse, Saul beheld a mysterious figure surrounded by brilliant light.

By this time the other men had come up to where Saul was lying on the road. "Who was that speaking?" one man asked.

"I heard a voice, too," exclaimed another rider, "but there is no one here except Saul." Quickly the men dismounted. Saul felt strong arms help him to his feet. Weakly he stretched out his hands in the direction of their voices.

"Saul, what is wrong?" one of his companions burst out, seeing him stumble and trip as he tried to walk.

"I am blind!" the young Hebrew cried. "Take me to Damascus!" In Damascus, Saul's companions took him to the home of one of his friends. An old man answered to their loud knocking.

"Does Judas live here?" they asked.

"Yes," answered the old man. "I am he. What do you want?"

Drawing Saul forward by the arm, the soldier introduced him: "This is Saul of Tarsus, who knows you."

"Saul of Tarsus, son of Torah?" asked the old Hebrew.

"Yes, yes," returned Saul, turning his face in the direction of Judas' voice.

"Welcome, Saul! I know your father well! Welcome to my home!"

"Thank you, Judas," Saul answered gratefully. "Thank you for receiving me."

"But what is the matter with you?" asked the old man as Saul slowly, weakly stepped toward him. "Are you sick?"

"I will tell you later," replied the young man. "Now I must have silence and rest."

Guided to a private upper room by his gracious host, Saul sank wearily onto the soft sheepskin mat, which served as a bed. Yes, silence and rest was what he needed. . . . During three days of quiet and rest, he slowly collected his thoughts. Alone in the room, he prayed, "Lord, what will you have me do?"

While Saul was at Judas' house, Jesus appeared to a Christian of Damascus named Ananias. "Go to the street called Straight," Jesus commanded. "There you will find in the house of Judas a young Hebrew from Tarsus, called Saul."

"But, Lord," protested Ananias, "I have heard from many Christians of the evil done by this man. He has killed many of the Christians of Jerusalem. Now he comes to arrest Your followers here in Damascus. . . ."

"Go!" Jesus replied. "I have chosen this man to carry My Name to the nations of the world."

Later that day, Judas heard a gentle knocking at his door. He opened to see Ananias. "I was told," the Christian explained politely, "that there is a man here named Saul. I would like to speak with him."

"Certainly," replied Judas, motioning for Ananias to enter. "Come right this way, please."

"Saul," Judas called softly as he entered the darkened room where the young man lay. "There is someone here to see you."

As Saul stood to greet his guest, Ananias embraced him, saying, "Saul, my brother, the Lord Jesus has sent me to you that you may see once again and be filled with the Holy Spirit."

"Then, my sins are forgiven?" Saul asked hopefully. In reply Ananias placed his hand upon Saul's dark head. Immediately there fell from Saul's eyes scale-like coverings.

"I can see!" the young man burst out joyfully. Gratefully he thanked Ananias and the two had a long talk together. Then Ananias baptized and confirmed Saul.

4

Escape to Jerusalem

Full of grace and zeal, Saul told the story of his conversion to the Christians of Damascus. "I came to persecute Christ," he admitted to the crowds standing in the great hall. "But now I have seen His power. He is truly the Lord, the Son of God!" Still, fear and doubt could be seen on the faces of many of the Christians listening to Saul.

"Is not this man the persecutor of the followers of Christ in Jerusalem?" one Christian whispered.

Another man spoke up, "Yes, he is the one! And he has come to arrest us Christians here in Damascus!" One by one people started to leave the room. Saul realized that they had not believed his story. Within a few minutes Saul stood alone in the empty hall. A great sorrow flooded his heart. He wanted so much to tell these people how good Jesus had been to him, but they refused to listen. . . .

Later, at the home of Ananias, Saul told his friend that the Christians doubted his conversion. "Do not be troubled, Saul," Ananias told him. "You must not blame the Christians for not believing your story right away. For weeks they have trembled, hearing tales of your cruelty to Christians at Jerusalem."

"Yes," Saul agreed sadly, "After what I have done, I cannot blame them for not trusting me."

"Give them a chance. They will come to believe you and love you," Ananias promised.

Back in Jerusalem the high priests listened with fury to the story of Saul's conversion. "To think I trusted him as one of our most zealous rabbis!" stormed Caiphas.

"How dare he turn from our religion to become a Christian!" burst out another high priest.

"We must kill him, before all the people follow his example!" cried another.

"Yes!" they all shouted together, "he must die!"

However before the high priests had time to carry out their evil plans, Saul made a long trip into the desert. Jesus inspired him to go there. For a long time he lived among the bare rocks and shifting sands. All that time he prayed and was taught many things by Jesus.

After three years Saul left the desert. How his heart burned with love as he tramped the winding trails to the city of Damascus. As he passed the ragged, dusty shepherds and the richly-dressed merchants, his heart filled with a great desire to bring all men—rich and poor—to the feet of Christ. Saul's eyes narrowed as he gazed on the bare, black hills in the distance. "Is that what Calvary looked like?" he wondered to himself. The thought of Calvary and of Jesus' death reminded Saul that he would have to suffer for Jesus as Jesus had suffered for him. "O Lord," he prayed, "make me strong enough to suffer something for your love."

Saul's trials began as soon as he entered Damascus. "You cannot stay here, Saul," his Christian friends exclaimed. "The high priests

Saul's friends helped him slip out of Damascus in a large trading basket.

of Jerusalem are still after you. Their men have been ordered to kill you on sight."

"That kind merchant who gave you a ride into Damascus on one of his camels saved your life, Saul," another man told him. "Even now, soldiers are on watch for you at the gates of the city."

"My friends," Saul answered bravely. "I have to escape from Damascus somehow. I must go to Jerusalem to see Peter!"

Very late that night all Damascus lay in darkness and silence. Three black figures slipped down the narrow streets to a deserted corner of the city. Quickly they ran up the outside stairway on the side of an abandoned mud brick house next to the city wall. When they reached the roof, another man stepped out of the shadows to greet them, "Good! At last you are here! I was getting worried. Ready, Saul?" he asked one of the three men.

"Ready to go—with the grace of God," Saul whispered back. "Where is the basket?"

"Right here," the fourth man answered. "Get in quickly and the three of us will lower you to the ground through this window in the city wall. We have to work fast before the guards see us."

Saul jumped into the huge basket and slowly, silently his friends lowered him through the opening in the great stone wall. When the basket hit the earth, Saul leaped out and gratefully waved good-bye to his friends. Then turning his face from Damascus, he set out on the long road to Jerusalem. There he would see Peter, who represented Jesus as the Head of the Church!

5

Barnabas Stands Up for Saul

Once in Jerusalem, Saul headed immediately for the home of a Christian. That night he spoke at a meeting of all the Christians. "I believe in Jesus because I saw Him!" he declared fervently to his listeners, crowded together in the small room. Then he told them the whole story of his meeting with Jesus, of his blindness, and of his baptism. "Now, my friends," he concluded, "I put myself entirely at your service and at the service of Christ! I want to do all I can to convert others to Him!"

Suspicion marked the faces of many of the Christians. Murmurs of doubt and distrust ran through the crowd. Seeing that a disagreement would break out, one of the Christians suggested that they close the meeting early. The others eagerly agreed, throwing dark looks at Saul. After a short prayer of closing, the men and women quickly filed out into the warm night.

Tremendous grief filled the heart of the great convert as he stood alone in the empty chamber. Neither the Christians, nor the Apostles themselves would believe in his conversion. Suddenly Saul felt a tap on his shoulder and realized he had not been left completely alone. He turned to face a tall, stout man, whose sandy hair matched his light brown eyes. A kindly smile lit up his tan face. He introduced himself: "Brother Saul, my name is Barnabas. I have heard much about you from my friends in Damascus."

The disciple's warm greeting melted the bitterness in Saul's heart. He clasped Barnabas' outstretched hand eagerly and said, "I am happy to meet you, Barnabas." The two talked together for several hours. Saul answered in detail all Barnabas' questions about his conversion.

He hoped this friendly disciple would convince the other Christians that he could be trusted.

Several days later Barnabas spoke with Peter and the other Apostles. "Saul is sincere. He really has given up his evil ways and wishes to preach about Jesus," Barnabas insisted.

James looked doubtfully at Peter. "Do you really think we can believe this Saul? I wonder if he is a spy of the high priests."

"We must give everyone a chance, James," Peter replied gently. "How many of us has the grace of God converted from sin? I think we should at least listen to his story."

Barnabas was happy that he had succeeded in convincing Peter to listen to Saul. Quickly he sent for him to come at once.

When Saul arrived, Peter welcomed him warmly. The two remained together for fifteen days. They spoke to each other of the teachings of Jesus and of His mercy. "I promised to love Him and never to desert Him," Peter recalled, shaking his head regretfully. "Then, three times I denied Him. . . ."

"And I," Saul replied, "arrested, imprisoned and killed His followers." For the rest of his life he wept for the cruel things he had done to the Christians.

To make up for his past sins, Saul longed with all his heart to preach the Christian faith to everyone. Even when he met his old schoolmates, now grown men, Saul could not resist telling them of Jesus. As the former students talked together in the public square, Saul could see that his listeners were not convinced.

"What you say is blasphemy!" one of them said sharply.

"No!" Saul cried. "You do not understand!" The others laughed mockingly.

"Saul, you are a fool!" one burst out.

"You poor man!" added another. "Have you, too, become a mad follower of this Crucified One?"

Later, Saul climbed the temple steps to pray. Inside the great main hall, he fell to his knees. How disappointed he was that his fellow Hebrews refused to listen to him!

Just then a beautiful white light shone in front of him. He looked up and with joy beheld his beloved Lord Jesus! "Leave this city as soon as possible," Jesus told him. "These people will not listen to your words. I wish to send you to faraway nations."

6

Saul Goes to Antioch of Syria

The next day he left for Tarsus. Back in his father's house once again, Saul worked for the conversion of his relatives and neighbors. Eagerly he told them of his conversion to Christianity. Many people of Tarsus believed Saul's story. They loved to hear him talk about Jesus and His goodness. "Tell us, more," they would beg when he finished speaking. "We want to know all about the Lord Jesus, too."

During these brief weeks, Saul also prayed much and planned how he would preach Jesus to the pagans.

Antioch in Syria was the second largest city of the Roman Empire. Full of shining marble temples and beautiful palaces, it was a glorious and famous city. Many fervent Christians lived there. Peter sent Saul's loyal friend, Barnabas to guide the Christians of Antioch. The zealous Barnabas worked very hard and made many more converts. Yet he could see that there was too much to be done for only one man. So he wrote to Saul: "Will you not come to Antioch, my brother? I need your help very much. Here many souls are eager to hear about Jesus!"

Glowing with zeal, Saul gladly departed for Antioch. He and Barnabas succeeded in converting many, many pagans to Jesus. About a year after Saul's arrival, a prophet called Agabus came to Antioch from Jerusalem. He foretold that a great famine soon would come over the entire world.

Not long after, news came from Jerusalem that many people there were starving to death. The generous converts at Antioch gathered together as much food as they could spare.

Saul and Barnabas then carried the precious grain and fruits to Jerusalem.

Meanwhile the Christians of Jerusalem were suffering not only hunger, but also the persecutions of King Herod Agrippa. This cruel ruler had ordered Christians to be whipped. Then he commanded his soldiers to behead James, brother of the Apostle John. St. Peter, too, was thrown into a dark, damp prison by Herod's men to await his death.

But God struck the evil king with a terrible sickness. Herod died eaten up by worms. God also sent an angel to free Peter from prison. When they saw him safe and sound, the Apostles rejoiced and thanked God for this new miracle. They knew Jesus was on their side. He would help them overcome every trouble in order to preach the true faith!

7

The Evil Magician

Closer and closer drew the hour in which Saul would begin his preaching to the whole world. One night while he was praying, his soul was lifted by God up to the third heaven. There Jesus told him many beautiful things. What he saw and heard was so wonderful that Saul could never explain it to anyone.

After Saul and Barnabas returned to Antioch, they were made bishops and sent by the Apostles on their first great mission to the pagans. Speedily they prepared to sail for the Island of Cyprus. The two waved good-bye to their dear friends from the deck of the ship.

Standing on the docks, the Christians shouted farewell to their beloved leaders. "Blessed are the feet of those who bring good news!" cried one of the converts.

"May the Lord Jesus go with you!" cried another, as the ship slowly pulled away from the city and headed toward the open sea.

Landing at Salamis, the capital of Cyprus, the two apostles were greeted by the disciple John Mark.

"Saul, this is my cousin," explained Barnabas, introducing John Mark. "Why not take him with us? I know he will be a great help." Saul looked searchingly at the tall, slender young man standing before him. The youth ran a work-roughened hand through his sandy hair. His blue eyes flashed eagerly as he a- waited Saul's answer. "The youth seems so zealous," Saul thought, "but will he be able to live our hard life?"

"Preaching to the pagans will not be easy, you know," Saul warned slowly.

"I know! I know!" John Mark returned quickly. "But I can take it!"

"Well, all right," Saul agreed. "Come with us, John Mark. We do need help."

After making many converts in Salamis, the three set out for Paphos, where the governor of the island lived. Climbing up and down steep mountain trails, the Apostles finally arrived at Paphos. The governor, Sergius Paulus, enjoyed learning about different religions. He was also studying magic under the guidance of a magician named Elymas.

When he heard about the three strangers who spoke of a new religion, he sent for them. As soon as the three were led into his study room, the governor asked them to speak.

Saul looked carefully at this tall, well-built official, so handsomely dressed in a white robe. Sergius Paulus was seated on a huge gold chair, behind a blue marble table covered with scrolls. He rested his ringed fingers upon the scrolls and said eagerly, "Tell me about this Jesus of whom you preach."

As Saul spoke to him, he could see the ruler's interest in Jesus growing. The governor did not move his brown eyes once from Saul's face. When Saul stopped for a minute to see what Sergius Paulus would say, the ruler burst out, "Tell me more! I enjoy hearing about Jesus! What else did He do?"

Fervently Saul continued. His heart overflowed with wonderful things to tell about Jesus! As he spoke he felt a tug on his robe. One of his companions was trying to tell him something. Saul shot a quick look at the far corner of the study. There behind the huge velvet curtain stood a dark figure listening. . . . Who was that? In an instant, the figure slipped out from behind the curtain and through a nearby side door. Saul began to suspect that something was up. Quickly he finished his talk and waited for Sergius Paulus to speak.

"Well said, my friends!" cried the governor warmly. "I am always ready to hear anyone speak on religion! How can you be so sure, though, that what Jesus taught is the true faith?"

"Because," Saul replied, "Jesus worked miracles to prove the truth of what he said."

"I have a magician in my household who can do very wonderful things," the ruler returned. Clapping his hands, he called for a slave. "Send the magician Elymas to me, at once," he ordered. The slave bowed and quickly left the room.

A few minutes later, a tall, thin old man entered the room. A jet-black cape fell from his shoulders to his toes and a strangely-shaped jewel hung from the fine silver chain around his neck.

"Elymas," Sergius Paulus explained, "these men have sailed here from Antioch. They have been telling me all about Jesus and the new Christian religion."

Elymas frowned at the Apostles. "Master," he addressed the governor, "I advise you to have no more to do with these foolish men. I know the crazy things they speak of—how a God came down from heaven in the form of a man—how this God died on the cross. What they say is nothing but lies and nonsense!"

Saul felt himself grow hot with anger. "How dare this man make fun of Jesus!" he thought fiercely to himself, throwing a bitter look at the magician.

"You had better send these men off the Island," warned Elymas boldly, "or they will have all your people following their foolish ideas."

"O full of evil and wickedness!" Saul burst out, stepping toward the magician. "Son of the devil! How dare you try to turn souls from the truth! Behold the hand of the Lord is upon you! For a time you shall be blind!"

"Help!" Elymas gasped, as everything went black before his eyes. Wildly he rubbed his face and strained to see with his now sightless eyes. "Help! I cannot see!"

Sergius Paulus leaped from his chair. "Saul! What did you do to the man?" he cried, half angry and half afraid.

"I did nothing," Saul answered gravely. "It is by the power of God that Elymas was blinded!"

"Then your religion must be from God!" Sergius Paulus whispered in amazement as he dropped back into his chair. "I must become a Christian!"

8

Trouble at
Antioch of Pisidia

Soon after the baptism of Sergius Paulus,
Saul and Barnabas and John Mark sailed from
Cyprus to the shores of Asia Minor. "There are
many souls waiting for us in this land," Saul
declared to his companions, as their ship docked
at the port city of Perge.

"I do not think I will be going with you,
Saul and Barnabas," John Mark told them sadly. "I feel very homesick. Let me visit my family

for a while. Then I will come and join you later." Saul looked at John Mark in disappointment.

"It would be better if he returned home. What do you think, Saul?" Barnabas said. Then he comforted his young cousin, saying, "Well, John Mark, I guess you found this apostolic life too hard. God must have other plans for you. Go home now and bring our greetings to the Christians there."

"Yes, the best thing is for him to turn back," Saul agreed softly. "I was afraid the boy was too weak in spirit to last," he thought. "As for Barnabas and myself, may we never give up preaching Christ to the world! With the grace of God, we will succeed! We will bring many souls to Jesus!"

After John Mark had left for Jerusalem, Saul and Barnabas, on mules, began the dangerous journey over the mountains to the city of Antioch of Pisidia. For many days they carefully guided their mules over narrow, rocky mountain paths. They kept a sharp lookout for bandits, who were known to hide in the hills, waiting to rob any passing traveler.

At last, the two tired Apostles arrived safely in Antioch. This Antioch was a different city from the one where they had stayed before.

In this Roman colony, Saul began using his Roman name of Paul, instead of the Hebrew, Saul.

The people in this city knew nothing about Christ. So Paul and Barnabas first spoke to the Hebrew people in the synagogue. "The Savior we have been awaiting for so many thousands of years has come!" Paul and Barnabas told the crowd in the synagogue. "He is Jesus of Nazareth, Who was crucified in order to save us from our sins!"

The Hebrews listened carefully, but most of them were not sure whether to believe the Apostles or not. To be polite, the leaders of the synagogue invited Paul and Barnabas to continue their preaching another time.

A week later the Apostles returned to the synagogue. By this time news of their preaching had spread all over the city. Hundreds of people, pagans as well as Hebrews, flocked to the synagogue to hear them. They converted many to Jesus. Full of fervor and thanksgiving, the new followers of Christ shouted, "Let us give glory to the Lord Who has created us for eternal life!"

The leaders of the synagogue became jealous of the Apostles' success. A few days after Paul and Barnabas had given their wonderful speeches in the synagogue, one of the new converts named Justus came to the house where they were staying. "Paul and Barnabas, you had better leave Antioch at once. The leaders of the synagogue plan to complain about you to the city rulers."

"But we did them no harm," Barnabas declared. "In fact, they themselves invited us to speak a second time in the synagogue."

"The chief leaders are stirring up trouble," Justus warned. "They have told the people that you and Paul are just making up stories and that you want to ruin the Hebrew religion."

Barnabas waited for Paul to speak. But Paul could only sigh in disappointment. Many had come to believe in Jesus since he and Barnabas had preached. But there were still many souls to be saved in Antioch! "Well," Paul replied at last, "perhaps we had better leave the city. I am not afraid of the synagogue leaders nor of the city rulers. But if we stay, it may mean trouble for the new converts."

"Yes," Barnabas agreed sadly, "we had better go. We must bring the message of Christ to many other people."

St. Paul's First Missionary Journey

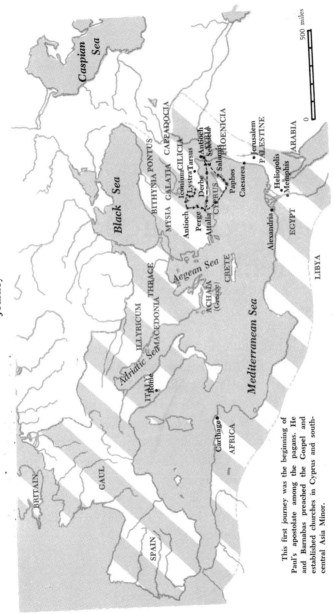

This first journey was the beginning of Paul's apostolate among the pagans. He and Barnabas preached the Gospel and established churches in Cyprus and south-central Asia Minor.

500 miles

9

The Courageous Thecla

That same afternoon Paul and Barnabas set out on foot for Iconium. When they were tired of walking, they rested for a while in the shade of a tree. After tramping many dusty miles, they reached Iconium at last. There they found many souls who eagerly listened to their words about Christ. Paul and Barnabas felt great happiness as their listeners cried, "Tell us more about Jesus!" "When can we be baptized?" "Do we have to wait long before becoming Christians?"

Among the many, many converts the Apostles made, the most important was Thecla. Thecla was the eighteen-year-old daughter of a very rich nobleman. She was small and slender and had long, black hair. Everywhere in Iconium she was famous for her beauty and goodness. She was also very smart and spent much time studying about different religions. Now Thecla was engaged to a young nobleman named Tamiridus. They were to be married soon.

Next to Thecla's house stood the home of Onesiforus, one of the new Christians. Paul and Barnabas often came to his house to teach their converts. Through the windows of her house, Thecla could hear Paul's fiery preaching. Wondering about this new religion, she listened closely to his words. Every time Paul preached to the Christians, she listened to him through the window.

One day she heard him speak on the beauties of virginity. Instead of marrying, a girl could remain a virgin and choose Jesus as her spiritual Bridegroom. Thecla was thrilled to hear about this spiritual marriage. Even though she was engaged to the handsome and rich Tamiridus, she was not happy. Something had seemed to be missing in her life. But now she felt she had found it. "I will break my engagement with Tamiridus. I will become a Christian and give myself entirely to Christ!" she decided.

Thecla told her parents of her desire to speak with Paul. But her father said sternly, "I forbid you to see that man! Anyway he is in prison so it is silly for you to try to talk with him."

Thecla would not give up. Early one morning she slipped out of the house with her jewel box hidden under her cloak. At the prison gates, she promised the guards some of her jewels if they would let her see Paul. The men greedily took the jewels and led her to the cell of the Apostle. There Paul told her more about Jesus. "It is wonderful to live for Christ!" he told her, "but you have to be strong. You must be ready to bear many sufferings for Jesus, your King."

"Oh yes, I am ready!" Thecla declared bravely.

Later that week Thecla and her family went to a big party. Tamiridus was also invited. The minute he saw Thecla, he happily rushed over to her. For the rest of the evening he gave her his complete attention. "My darling," the young noble told her, "the days before our marriage do not pass swiftly enough! Let us be married sooner."

Thecla did not know what to answer him. "How can I tell him that I want to become a Christian?" she asked herself. "How can I explain that I want to give myself to God alone?"

Then a thought came to her. "Oh Tamiridus, please forgive me, but parting from my parents is so hard! I would break their hearts if I were to be married sooner." To please his bride-to-be, the young man agreed to keep the first wedding date.

Again and again Thecla visited Paul. One day he told her she was ready for baptism. What a wonderful day for Thecla! After her baptism, her heart overflowed with new love and courage. "As soon as possible," she decided, "I must tell Tamiridus that I wish to break our engagement."

A few days later Tamiridus came to visit her. Drawing him aside, Thecla said sorrowfully, "Tamiridus, I must tell you something."

"Yes, yes, what is it?" he asked gently.

"I . . . we . . . I wish to break our engagement. I do not feel ready for marriage."

"But, Thecla," the nobleman protested, "I have waited so long. . . ."

"I am sorry, but our marriage cannot take place!" Thecla replied firmly. Disturbed and unhappy, Tamiridus left Thecla's house. He could not understand what had come over the young woman. But he clung to the hope that she would change her mind.

That same week, Thecla, as she had done so many times before, slipped away from home to see Paul. He was still in prison. But since she paid the guards well, they permitted her to see him. With her heart burning within her, she listened to Paul speak. She never tired of hearing about Jesus.

Just then Thecla's mother and Tamiridus burst into the room. "So here you are!" shouted Tamiridus. "Talking with this faker!"

"You are a disgrace to our family, Thecla," her mother scolded. Thecla grew afraid and confused. She looked at Paul.

"Go, my daughter, go," he told her. "Be strong! I will pray for you!"

"Your punishment is coming, too!" Tamiridus shouted fiercely at Paul.

Then taking Thecla aside, Tamiridus demanded, "Thecla, do you really believe this man's lies?"

"What Paul says is not a lie!" declared Thecla. "He preaches about the true God."

"Have you become a follower of his? Are you what they call a 'Christian'?" he asked sternly.

"Yes, yes I am a Christian," she admitted, trembling. "I have given myself to Christ and I wish to be His alone."

"Forget this religion! Say you will be mine!" begged Tamiridus.

"No!" Thecla answered. "I belong to Jesus!"

"All right, then," the nobleman snapped, "you will die!" Still she would not give in. Angry at her refusal to marry him, Tamiridus ordered the guards to take Paul and her before the judge.

Without mercy, the pagan judge ordered Paul to be whipped and Thecla to be burned alive in front of the prison. A great crowd gathered to see the death of this beautiful young girl who refused to give up Christ. Thecla was tied to the stake. The guards set fire to the piles of wood at her feet. She was very frightened, but she prayed, "O God, give me strength. Help me to suffer any pain rather than be unfaithful to you."

The flames shot up in front of the girl. Then from the sky burst a clap of thunder and a downpour of rain which completely put out the fire! Thecla was saved! Terrified by this wonder, the crowd rushed away from the prison.

But her trials were not yet over. She was sent to Antioch to be tried by the governor. One look at the beautiful Thecla, and he fell in love with her. "Marry me, Thecla," he pleaded. "You are the only one who can make me happy. Say you will be mine and I will take you away from this terrible prison."

"No!" she answered firmly. "I have already given myself to Another—to a King Who awaits me in heaven!"

"Forget this foolish religion! Be my wife. I will make you the happiest woman in the world!" declared the governor.

"Only Jesus can make me truly happy!" replied Thecla.

"You will change your mind. I know you will," the governor told her as the guards led her away. For the next week, the governor spoke with her every day, begging her to marry him. His constant asking for her hand, made Thecla all the stronger in her refusals. The governor's love for her began to turn to hatred. At last, furious because she would not marry him, the governor had her thrown to the lions.

As she waited for the hungry beasts to tear her to pieces, Thecla bravely prayed, "O Lord, I am happy to die for You Who died for me!" What was her surprise to see the lions curl up tamely at her feet instead of clawing her to bits!

The governor stared in amazement. Still he did not give up his evil plans. "Either she marries me or she shall die!" he snarled to himself.

So he ordered Thecla to be thrown into the poison snake pit. But not one of the ugly creatures touched God's heroine. "You are all powerful, O Lord!" she breathed gratefully. "You have saved me from death!" Frightened by her victory over the snakes, the governor set her free.

After staying with the Christians for a while, Thecla went to live near Iconium. Her wisdom and zeal drew many souls to Christ. Until her death at ninety years of age, Thecla continued to bring people to the feet of her divine Bridegroom. The Church calls her the first woman martyr. She is called a martyr even though she died a natural death, because she suffered so much for her faith. St. Thecla's feastday is September 23rd.

10

The Stoning of Paul and Barnabas

By the time Thecla was free, Paul had escaped from prison. He and Barnabas then set out for Lystra. When they arrived, they began to preach Christ to whoever would listen to them. Within a few days, they had made a large number of converts.

Then, one day, the Apostles began to speak in the market place for the first time. A good-sized crowd gathered around them. Among the richly-robed merchants and the poorly-dressed shepherds, Paul noticed a ragged looking fellow sitting in a corner. He glanced at the man's feet and saw that they were twisted and bent so he could not walk. An old, worn crutch lay across his lap. However, joy and faith shone on the poor beggar's face as he drank in Paul's words.

Suddenly the Apostle cried out, "In the Name of Jesus, stand up on your feet. Your faith has cured you!" At once the man stood up and looked at his feet. No longer crooked, they were perfectly straight and normal!

"I can walk!" he burst out joyfully. "Thank you. Thank you!" he sobbed, throwing himself on his knees before Paul and Barnabas.

The crowds gasped in amazement. This stranger had cured a cripple! "They are gods!" one man shouted.

"The gods have visited us!" cried another. "Bring out the bulls! We must offer sacrifices to them!"

"He is the god Mercury!" someone declared, falling on his knees in front of Paul.

"Stop it!" the Apostle burst out in horror. He pulled the man to his feet. "I am no god!"

"This one is Jupiter, king of the gods!" cried another person, pointing at Barnabas.

65

The excited pagans brought bulls to sacrifice to Paul and Barnabas, but the two Apostles protested in horror.

"No!" Barnabas shouted. "You deceive yourselves!"

But it was too late. The priest from the temple of Jupiter had already arrived at the square. His helpers dragged huge bulls wreathed with flowers behind them. "They are gods! They are gods!" the people shouted with one voice. "Make ready the sacrifices!"

"Stop!" burst out Paul and Barnabas together. "We are not gods! We are men, like yourselves! We have come to preach the true God Who made heaven and earth!" With that they rushed into the crowd and tried to push the people away from the bulls.

Just as the high priest was about to plunge his knife into one bull's breast, Paul grabbed his hand. "Stop this foolishness! Listen to us and be converted to the true God!" he cried.

In the midst of the wild shouts and uproar of the people, several strangers arrived. They were the enemies of Paul and Barnabas from Antioch and Iconium. Discovering that the two Apostles were in the middle of the confusion, they saw their chance to get them into trouble.

One of these wicked men slipped up to the high priest and pulled him aside to whisper excitedly, "You should drive those two men out of your city . . . even stone them! They will only cause you a lot of trouble!"

Behind the two, a voice cried, "But these men cured me. They must be good!" It was the cripple.

"Quiet you!" burst out the high priest angrily. "We should be thankful that this man has told us the truth about these deceivers."

Then waving his hands in the air, the high priest got the attention of most of the noisy crowd. "Stone those two strangers!" he shouted, pointing to Paul and Barnabas. "They are fakers!" The people were so excited they were ready to do anything, no matter how senseless or unjust. So, snatching big rocks from the street, the men wildly threw them at the Apostles. The two covered their heads with their cloaks and tried to run away. Barnabas escaped and ran for help.

But the crowd overpowered Paul. Cut and bruised, he fell onto the dusty street. The mob hurled stones at him and then, thinking he was dead, they dragged him outside the city gates and left him in a heap on the ground.

By the time the crowd was gone, Barnabas arrived with some of the disciples. He, too was wounded, but not as badly as Paul. He and the other disciples began to carry Paul away when they heard voices.

"Look, Mother! Look at the men over there! They are carrying someone!" Barnabas and the disciples looked up to see a young lad about sixteen years old running toward them.

Behind the boy came an older woman. "Why, the man is all covered with blood!" she burst out as she reached Barnabas and the others.

"He is badly wounded," Barnabas explained.

"Timothy," the woman said to the boy, "bring us some water to wash the man's wounds. Be sure no one sees you, though."

"I am Eunice," she introduced herself after the boy left. "You are Barnabas and this is Paul. Am I right? My mother, my son, and myself have become followers of Jesus because of you."

Night had fallen by the time Timothy returned. Eunice quickly washed Paul's wounds. Then Barnabas, Timothy, and the other disciples carried him to Eunice's house. Lying on a warm mat, Paul began to recover. "Do not worry, Paul," Barnabas comforted him. "We are among friends."

"Thanks be to God," breathed Paul. "Now I feel much better. The Lord saved me." After a few days of the kindly care of Eunice and her mother, Lois, Paul was completely cured. Then he and Barnabas left Lystra for Derbe.

On the way to Derbe, Paul kept thinking of Timothy. What a great help he was to Eunice. The tall, broad-shouldered boy was always busy doing errands for her. Paul remembered the steady, clear look in Timothy's blue eyes. He thought of the warm smile that often flashed in the boy's tan face.

"You know, Barnabas," Paul told his companion as they strode along. "I like that boy, Timothy. I would not be surprised if someday he does great things for God."

"He admires you, very much, you know, Paul," Barnabas returned. "I could not help overhearing him talking to his mother about you."

After making many converts at Derbe, the Apostles returned to Lystra, Iconium, and Antioch of Pisidia. At each city, they appointed leaders to guide the new converts.

Finally Paul and Barnabas sailed back to Antioch of Syria. They had been away from this city for about four years. What a joyful welcome the Christians gave the pair when they reached Antioch! Happy to be home again, Paul and Barnabas rejoiced with their people.

A few days later, however, Paul heard complaints about his missionary trip to the pagans. "Do you know what they are saying about us, Paul?" Barnabas asked him. "Some of the Hebrew Christians think we did wrong because we did not make the pagans practice the Law of Moses."

"I must go to see Peter," Paul replied. "I will tell him all about our travels. He is the head of the Church. If he agrees with what we did, then we did the right thing."

Soon after, Paul traveled to Jerusalem to see Peter. He explained everything he and Barnabas had done on their missionary trips. Peter shook Paul's hand warmly, "God was with you both and helped you make so many converts. I approve with all my heart of what you and Barnabas did."

11

Timothy Follows Paul

Even though he had just returned from a long missionary journey, Paul deeply longed to start out on another great missionary trip. This time he took Silas with him, instead of Barnabas. Silas was about as tall as Paul. He had curly brown hair and friendly brown eyes. Paul could see by his big, rough hands that Silas was used to hard work. Silas wanted very much to win souls for Christ, so he was delighted to go with Paul.

The two returned to Lystra. There they joyfully greeted Eunice, Lois, and Timothy. "Well, Timothy!" Paul declared, clapping his hand on the young man's shoulder, "you are quite a man, now!"

"Oh yes, Paul!" Timothy agreed, pleased at Paul's remark. "And I would like to come with you to preach about Jesus!"

"Very well, if your Mother agrees, you may come!" Paul replied.

Eunice very gladly agreed to let Timothy go with Paul and Silas. "I know you love Timothy like a father, Paul," she told the Apostle. "And I feel honored that my son wants to spend his life working for Christ."

Several weeks later, the two Apostles and Timothy departed for Galatia. The people of that country gave them a hearty welcome. These good souls joyfully heard the Apostles' words and soon became followers of Christ.

They loved Paul in a special way since he was the most zealous preacher of the three. "Paul, you are an angel of the Lord!" one of the new converts declared. "God sent you to us to preach about His Son." In fact, the Galatians loved and admired Paul so much that they would have given him their very eyes.

After leaving Galatia, Paul and his companions made their way to Troas. There a doctor visited Paul who often suffered from attacks of fever. This doctor, a Christian named Luke, was very pleased to meet the Apostle. Through the meeting with Paul, Luke became an even more fervent follower of Jesus. All during his life he greatly admired Paul. In fact, he wrote about many of Paul's adventures in the "Acts of the Apostles." Luke is also the author of one of the Gospels.

12

The Girl Possessed by a Devil

One night as Paul lay sleeping in Troas he had a strange dream. "Cross the sea and come to Macedonia," a man was begging him. "We need your help." Paul shook himself awake, "Jesus must be inspiring me through this dream," he thought. "It must be God's will that we preach to those people."

"Tomorrow," he decided, "we will sail to Macedonia in Europe!"

Paul and his fellow Apostles left the ship at the port of Neapolis in Europe. They made their way by boat to Philippi, a city of Macedonia.

The first convert Paul made in this city was Lydia, a seller of dyes. Very honest and good, Lydia had been seeking the truth about God for a long time. She listened to Paul with great interest. When he finished talking to her and the other people with her, Lydia asked him, "Paul, I would be very pleased to have you and your companions as my guests. People very often come to visit me. So at my house you would be able to preach to many souls."

"We will be glad to come!" Paul answered gratefully. "May God bless you for your kindness."

There was another woman in Philippi whom Paul drew to Christ. This poor creature was a slave girl, called the "Pythoness." A devil lived in her soul and gave her the power to foretell the future. Her evil masters dragged the ragged girl about the city streets with them. People paid much money to these men to hear the "Pythoness" tell their fortunes.

One day as Paul and Silas were walking through the public square, they saw this poor slave girl running after them. "These men are servants of the most high God," the girl screamed to the crowds as she pointed wildly at the Apostles. "They preach to you the way of salvation!"

"Paul, there is something wrong with her!" Silas whispered. The girl pulled furiously at her long, snarled hair and kept screaming.

"It is the devil!" Paul returned angrily. "He is in her soul!" Quickly Paul reached out and seized the girl by the arm. He looked straight into her stormy, black eyes. "In the Name of Jesus Christ, I command you to leave her!" he shouted to the devil. Instantly, the girl became calm. Peace filled her eyes and the wild look left her face.

She fell to her knees and whispered a soft "Thank you" to Paul.

The Apostle helped her to her feet and said gently, "Go in peace, my daughter." Pulling her rags around her thin shoulders, the girl slipped away.

Suddenly two angry men burst through the crowd and shouted at Paul and Silas, "What have you done with our slave? Where is she? We shall complain to the city rulers about you!" Then seizing Paul and Silas by the arms the men forced the Apostles to come with them to the house of the city rulers.

Surrounded by a restless, angry mob, the masters of the slave girl loudly declared that Paul and Silas were stirring up trouble. These two evil men said nothing about the slave girl. They knew Paul had every right to help her. So to make sure Paul and Silas would be punished the men accused them of being disloyal to Rome.

"You know it is against the law to preach a new religion without permission from Rome!" one of the men cried.

"These men are telling the people not to worship our Roman gods!" his partner screamed.

Philippi was under Roman rule, so the governors of the place forced everyone to bow to Roman authority. Paul and Silas tried to defend themselves, but the rulers would not listen. They frowned at the sight of the screaming men and restless crowds before them. Had the two strangers caused all this trouble? A good whipping would teach them a lesson!

The guards stripped Paul and Silas and cruelly whipped them. Then they chained Christ's Apostles to the damp, black walls of an underground prison cell. The jailor of the prison was ordered to keep a special watch over these "dangerous" prisoners.

79

Paul and Silas were not sad, however. "We should rejoice, Silas," Paul told his companion. "God has found us worthy to suffer something for His sake."

"You are right, Paul," Silas returned. "Let us sing something to praise Him!" The other prisoners stopped groaning and rattling their chains when they heard the Apostles singing. They were amazed. How could anyone be happy in this horrible prison?

Suddenly a great rumbling shook the prison. Huge cracks split the walls of the cells. "An earthquake!" Silas cried.

"Look, my brother!" Paul burst out joyfully. "My chains are broken. And the cell door has broken open. We are free!"

"An angel of the Lord has visited us," Silas breathed gratefully.

On a higher floor in the prison the jailer felt the rolling of the earth. Quickly he dashed down the stone stairway to the underground cells. In horror, he saw the cell doors hanging open. "If the prisoners escape, the rulers will have me killed," he groaned to himself. "It is better for me to die right now!"

So saying, he pulled out his knife. As he was about to plunge it into his heart, Paul cried out, "Stop! Do not harm yourself! We are all here!"

In amazement the jailer dropped his knife and went over to Paul. "But the door is open! Your chains are broken! Why did you not save yourself?"

"It is you who are going to save yourself," Paul replied gently. "Believe in the Lord Jesus Christ and you and your whole family will be saved."

Then the jailer and his family (who lived in the rooms above the prison) cared for the wounds of Paul and Silas. The two Apostles told them all about Jesus and baptized them.

Meanwhile, Timothy, Lydia, and some of her powerful friends went to the city rulers. "Do you realize," one of the men angrily told the chief ruler, "that those two men you ordered beaten and imprisoned yesterday are Roman citizens. It is against the law to punish a Roman citizen without proper trial."

"Roman citizens!" the chief ruler exclaimed in fear. "But we did not know that!" Instantly they sent a letter by way of a slave to the jailer. The letter told the jailer to free Paul and Silas at once.

81

"Paul," cried the jailer, when he finished reading the message, "you and Silas are free to go! The rulers just sent me these orders."

"No indeed!" was Paul's quick answer. "Although we are Roman citizens, we were beaten and imprisoned without a trial. The rulers treated us shamefully in public. Now they want to free us in secret, do they?! Nothing doing! Let them come themselves to free us!"

"Paul is right!" Silas added. "We are glad to offer our sufferings to God. But we must have respect from the people, too. Otherwise we will not be able to bring them to Christ. By freeing us in public, the rulers will show the people that we are not troublemakers, but honest men!"

Shaking with fear, the city rulers came themselves to free them. They led Paul and Silas to the public square to show everyone that the Apostles had been unfairly treated. Then they begged them to leave the city before any more trouble started. This the Apostles did. They only wished to leave everyone in peace.

St. Paul's Second Missionary Journey

On his second journey, Paul revisited some of his churches in Asia and continued on into the country of the Galatians and Mysians. From Troas he crossed over into Europe and established churches in Macedonia and Greece. He also founded a church at Ephesus.

13

The Students Laugh at Paul

The port of Thessalonica was the next stop on the Apostles' journey. There the three missionaries stayed with the tentmaker, Jason.

Besides preaching, Paul worked hard at tentmaking. While he wove the heavy goats hair into strong tents, he would speak of Jesus to the dock-workers, sailors, and other workmen around him. These rough and ready fellows were easily won to Christ because of Paul. They admired him for working as hard as they did.

Paul and his companions made many converts in Thessalonica. Still, there were those who were jealous of Paul's success. These wicked people got Paul into so much trouble that Jason had to pay a big fine to the city rulers.

After that the Apostles left Thessalonica and went to another city, Beroea. Their enemies from Thessalonica followed them to Beroea and made more trouble for the Apostles.

Paul escaped to Athens. How sad he felt to leave Timothy and Silas behind in Beroea. He was also sorry to leave his many new converts. "O Lord," he prayed, as he walked along the sea road toward Athens, "someday let me see again the faces of my dear sons."

Finally Paul reached the beautiful and famous city of Athens. Everywhere he looked, he saw shining white temples and tall marble statues of false gods. The Greeks offered sacrifices to the gods on the beautiful altars in front of the statues. Suddenly one of the altars caught Paul's eye. A sign on it read, "To the Unknown God."

In the public square, the Apostle saw many students and teachers standing around and talking. He went up to one of the students and began a discussion about religion. The other students, being very proud, looked down on Paul.

"Who is that strange man?" one of them asked.

"Some sort of magician, I think," replied his friend.

"Listen to the queer things he is saying, will you?" the first young man said, making fun of Paul.

Meanwhile, Paul made believe he had not heard their remarks. He kept talking with the first student he had met. Finally the young Greek told him, "Come to the Areopagas on the Hill of Mars, tomorrow, Paul. There you can tell us more about this God Who came down from heaven and became a man."

Shouts of laughter arose from the other students. Paul, however, refused to let anything stop him from preaching Christ. "I will be glad to come and talk," he replied warmly.

The next morning Paul climbed the steep street to the Areopagas, a flat open space overlooking the city and the sea. All the students and teachers gathered around Paul as he stood to speak. "Men of Athens! I see that you are the most religious of people. Passing through the streets of your city, I saw an altar honoring 'The Unknown God.' I wish to tell you about

this known God. He is Jesus Christ Who was crucified for our sins and three days later rose from the dead!"

The words about Jesus' resurrection from the dead made the Athenians laugh. "You are crazy!" one of the men cried, shaking his head in disgust.

"Rise from the dead? Who can believe such a thing?" another man burst out.

"We will hear you another time!" a third Athenian mocked.

In a few seconds, the entire crowd had melted away, leaving Paul alone. "They refused to hear the Word of God," Paul said sadly to himself, gazing at the blue sea dancing in the morning sun. "Everywhere the pagans listened to our message—at Antioch, Iconium, Lystra, Derbe, Philippi, Thessalonica, and Beroea. But at Athens they only laugh...."

Suddenly a voice interrupted his thoughts: "Are you Paul of Tarsus?" The Apostle turned to see a dark-haired young Greek striding toward him. The stranger was followed by a woman, robed in white.

"Yes," Paul answered politely, now facing the couple. "What can I do for you?"

"Your words," the man declared eagerly, "were for us words of life! We wish to follow you! I am Dionysius and this is Damaris, a woman of Athens."

"We want to hear more about this Jesus," the woman added fervently. "I wish to give myself entirely to His service."

By this time a few other Greeks, breathless from climbing the hill, arrived. Their dark eyes flashed with interest as they listened to Dionysius and Damaris. "We want to follow Christ, too! Please, tell us more about Him!" they begged.

"Thanks be to God!" breathed Paul in wonder. Joyfully he began teaching these Greeks all about Jesus. "Even if the others laughed at me, with God's help, I can bring these good men and women to follow Him." Paul thought gratefully.

14

Corinth — City of Wealth and Fun — Won Over by Paul

From Athens he walked many dusty, weary miles to Corinth. Built on the shores of the deep blue Aegean Sea, the city of Corinth overflowed with merchants, soldiers, craftsmen, and shop keepers. From all over the Roman empire, people came to enjoy themselves in this beautiful, rich and fun-loving city. As Paul entered, he was pleased to see people from every part of Europe and Asia Minor. "All of these people can carry the Word of God back to their own countries," he thought to himself.

Dock workers, unloading a cargo ship, were not too busy to notice Paul. "Who is that stranger over there?" one of them asked his companion, as the two strained to lift a heavy box of fruit.

"Oh, just another seeker of good fortune!" replied the other scornfully.

However, within a few months, Paul had made many converts. He worked day and night, in houses and on the streets to preach Christ. Timothy and Silas soon joined Paul here. The three Apostles had great success in teaching the Word of God to the Corinthians.

These people loved fun and merriment. They were always ready for a good time. Often they fell into sin because they were too eager for pleasure. But unlike the proud Athenians, the warm-hearted Corinthians listened to Paul and his companions. They changed their bad lives and followed Christ with great love and fervor.

"Where do you live? I want to ask you some questions about this Jesus," a young man asked Paul.

"At the home of the tentweavers, Aquila and Priscilla," Paul replied. "Come anytime. I will be glad to talk with you." Nearly everyday Paul met persons–like this young man–interested in Jesus. The house of Aquila and Priscilla often overflowed with strangers, eager to hear the Gospel.

Preaching the Word of God kept Paul very busy. But even so, he insisted on helping Aquila weave tents. "Why do you refuse the money and gifts the Christians offer you?" Aquila asked Paul one day. "The preacher has a right to make a living by preaching the Gospel, just as the workman earns a living by doing his trade."

"Of course, you should earn a living by preaching the Word of God!" Priscilla declared. "Is not that what Moses did—and Jesus, too!"

"No," Paul answered as his quick fingers worked the weaving loom, "I do not want the Christians to trouble themselves about me. I would rather earn my living with my own two hands."

Paul had enemies at Corinth, too. They were determined to get rid of the Apostle. One day these evil men gathered their courage. They seized Paul while he was preaching in one of the city streets and dragged him before the ruler, Gallio. "This man is speaking against the Roman empire," one of them cried.

"He ought to die!" another man shouted.

The Roman ruler, Gallio, was not so easily fooled. He realized the men were only jealous of Paul's success in making converts. "Let the man go!" he ordered sharply, waving his hand toward Paul. "I have nothing to do with matters of religion!"

So Paul was free once more to bring souls to Christ! To work for God was the greatest joy in Paul's life. Often he did penance so that people would turn from a life of sin to a life of goodness. Paul went without eating the foods he liked. When he felt tired, he did not complain. He offered his tiredness up to God. When he felt like sleeping, he forced himself to pray better and to work harder. For the love of God, he was happy to be poor and without many comforts.

Paul's favorite virtue was the love of his neighbors. He wished all of his spiritual children to practice this virtue. "Remember what Jesus said to the Apostles," he would tell his converts. "He said, 'Love one another as I have loved you.'"

Paul and his companions remained in Corinth for a long time. The people of the city were very dear to Paul's heart. He hated to leave them. But for Jesus he was ready to make any sacrifice. "I must go to other lands and countries," he declared firmly to his people. "There are still many souls waiting to hear about Christ!"

15

"Just a Piece
of His Cloak..."

Paul, Timothy, and Silas first returned to
Jerusalem to report to Peter about their work.
After staying a few weeks there, Paul decided
to go to Ephesus, another city on the shores of
the Aegean Sea. Timothy went with him. This
would be Paul's third missionary journey.

He found this great city full of all kinds of
people. Merchants, artists, workmen, students
and many others came to hear him preach the
Gospel.

Paul taught at the school of Tyrannus every day. Usually he sat on a mat with the scrolls of the Bible in front of him. All around him were gathered people eager to hear the Word of God.

Through Paul, God worked many wonders. One day through the windows of his house a very sick man watched Paul preaching in the street. For many years the man had lain ill, unable even to sit up. "So that is the great Apostle I have heard so much about," he sighed to himself. "If only I could touch the hem of his robe, I know I would be cured of this sickness."

He called his daughter. "Child", he told the girl, as he pointed out the window, "do you see that man with a green cloak—the one preaching to all those people? Go, and ask him to come here, my daughter. Tell him I know he can cure me from this sickness!"

Quickly the girl ran from the house. Her father's loving eye watched her as she slipped through the crowd and tried to get the apostle's attention. It was impossible. People were shouting questions at Paul from all sides. They pressed tightly against each other in order to get a better look at him. The girl was desperate. Her father had to get better! "Maybe just a

St. Paul's Third Missionary Journey

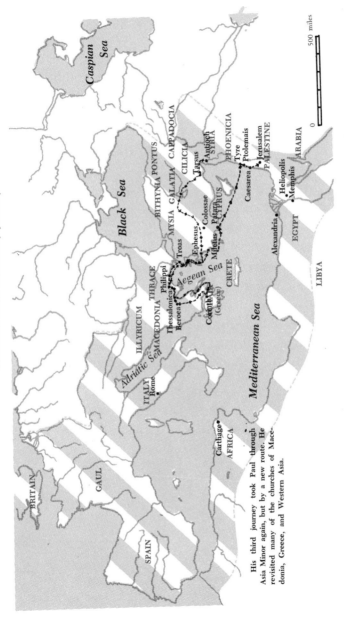

His third journey took Paul through Asia Minor again, but by a new route. He revisited many of the churches of Macedonia, Greece, and Western Asia.

piece of his cloak would be enough. . . . " she said to herself. Reaching between two women, she snatched a corner of Paul's cloak and tore it off! Clutching the precious scrap of material to her breast, she made her way through the masses of people to her house.

"Father!" she cried breathlessly, running up the stairs, "see what I have!" She waved the torn piece of Paul's cloak in his face. Seeing the man's surprised look, the girl explained, "It is a piece of his cloak, Father! This will be enough to cure you!"

In amazement at his daughter's idea, the man reached out and touched the cloth. Instantly he felt a thrill of strength run through his whole body. "I am cured!" he burst out, sitting straight up in bed. So holy was Paul, that even a piece of his cloak was enough to work a miracle!

16

Danger at Ephesus

Paul always showed great courage and strength in the face of any trouble. At the same time he had a very loving heart. He looked upon all his converts as his spiritual children.

For many months Paul had been away from Corinth. He knew how careless the Corinthians were. One day two servants of Chloe, a rich Christian woman of Corinth, came to Ephesus. They told Paul that many Corinthians had gone back to their pagan way of life. "My unfaithful sons and daughters of Corinth must correct themselves," Paul sighed to himself. "Since I cannot visit them now, I will send them a letter."

Paul's hands were so rough and stiff from tentmaking that he could no longer write. So he asked one of his friends to write the letter for him. "Tell the Corinthians," Paul began "that I scold them for their sins not out of anger and bitterness, but out of love. I do not think of them as bad sinners, but as my dear children. . . ."

Paul sent the letter to Corinth. He prayed that with God's help, his words would make his unfaithful converts give up their sins. He also sent Timothy to that city to remind the Corinthians of all that he, Paul, had taught them. Later, Paul made Timothy Bishop of Ephesus.

The Apostle wrote letters to his converts in the other cities he had visited. We still read his beautiful letters today. They are called the "Epistles of St. Paul."

*　*　*

Paul preached with such zeal in Ephesus that he convinced even the magicians to give up their black magic. These men were not or-

dinary magicians. No! They were helpers of the devil! They knew how to do many evil things. All the people feared them very much.

One day all of them gathered together around Paul in the public square. They had brought with them all their books on magic. One of the leaders explained to Paul: "We want to make up for our past sins. So we will burn all our books on black magic."

Paul was very pleased that these men wanted to become good. "God will bless you for giving up your evil ways," he told them.

Then the men piled all their books in the center of the square. With a flaming torch, Paul set fire to them. Great streaks of red shot up into the air as the books burned. "May a great fire of love for You burn in the hearts of these men, O Lord!" Paul prayed, as he watched the evil writings go up in smoke.

❖   ❖   ❖

Every year in the month of May, the Ephesians celebrated the feast of the pagan goddess, Diana. Many people who worshipped Diana came from the little towns outside of Ephesus.

In front of her temples, silver-workers shouted: "Buy your silver statues of Diana here! Get them now!" "Take home a beautiful statue of the great goddess!" Many of the travelers and city people eagerly bought the little silver statues of Diana. The silver-workers were very pleased. They made much money during the month of May.

This May, however, the silver business was very poor. Very few people wanted the statues. Paul had converted many of the Ephesians to Christianity. In disgust, the people of Ephesus told the silver-workers, "You cannot fool us! There is no such person as this Diana! We believe in Christ and worship the true God!"

One of the richest silver-workers, named Demetrius, became very angry. His silver business was failing day by day. He gathered all his fellow silver-workers together in his shop. Standing on a chair, he declared loudly, "That man Paul has ruined our business! He tells the people that our goddess does not exist!"

"He ought to be stoned!" cried one of the workers, shaking his fist.

"He must die!" thundered another. "How dare he speak against our great goddess?"

In one voice all the men shouted, "Great is Diana of the Ephesians!"

Then with a thunder of running feet, they rushed out of Demetrius' shop. Demetrius led them. "There are some of Paul's friends," he cried pointing at two men in the street. "Get them!" In an instant, the mob surrounded the poor men and dragged them to the public open-air theater.

Paul was preaching only a few streets away from the theater. He broke off in the middle of his speech as he heard all the noise. "What is that shouting and screaming for?" he asked his listeners.

Suddenly a man all splashed with mud pushed his way through the crowd. "Paul!" he cried, gasping for breath. "Your friends, Caius and Aristarchus—Demetrius and the silver-workers dragged them to the theater! I tried to stop them, but I could not! All the silver-workers are furious! They say you have spoiled their business by preaching about Christ!"

"I must go and explain to them!" Paul declared, rushing forward.

"No, Paul!" his listeners shouted, pulling him back. "It is too dangerous! That mob will kill you!"

"At all costs, I must preach the Gospel!" Paul answered, struggling to free himself from their grasp.

"Please, Paul, listen to us! Those silver-workers are crazy with anger! They will never listen to you!" one of the men cried.

"If you die now, think of all the other souls you will miss. If you do not preach to them, they may never hear about Christ!" burst out another man.

The mention of other souls still waiting to hear about Christ stopped Paul. "How many thousands of people still live in spiritual darkness," he thought to himself. "Yes, I must preach Christ to them!"

"You are right, my friends," he said slowly to his listeners. "I had better not go to the theater."

"In fact, Paul, the best thing for you is to leave Ephesus for a while," said the man who had brought the news.

"I know that Demetrius!" another man from the crowd added. "He stops at nothing to get rid of his enemies! He may well try to kill you himself!"

Meanwhile one of the city rulers, learning of the disorder in the theater, went there to speak to the crowds. He convinced them to go home and told Demetrius to bring his complaints against Paul to the proper authorities. So Caius and Aristarchus were freed.

105

Paul thanked the Lord that his friends had escaped harm. Then, realizing the wisdom of the Christians' advice, he left Ephesus. The ship slowly pulled away from the city. Paul watched as the buildings grew smaller and smaller and finally melted out of his sight. He felt sad to leave his many friends. But his heart rejoiced at the thought of so many Ephesians who were now followers of Christ!

17

Paul — Man of Miracles

From Ephesus, Paul went to Philippi. There Titus, one of his old friends, was the leader of the Christians. "Titus, my son!" Paul greeted the apostle warmly. "I am so happy to see you! Tell me, do you know if the Corinthians listened to my letter? Have they given up their sinful ways yet?"

"Yes, Paul," Titus assured him. "Your letter made the Corinthians see how they were offending God. They have done much penance for their sins!"

"Thanks be to God!" exclaimed Paul. "I must send them another letter. I will tell my sons and daughters how happy I am that they obeyed my advice. Soon I will go to see them."

A few weeks later, Paul did go to Corinth. After a three months stay in that city, he wished to sail for Jerusalem. But he heard that his enemies planned to drown him. So he journeyed on foot to Troas. After weeks of walking, he finally reached the city. Here he worked another of his miracles.

One Sunday night, he was preaching to the Christians of Troas. They were gathered around him in a third story room in the home of one of the converts. They knew he planned to leave the city the next morning. So every time Paul tried to call the meeting to a close, the Christians begged him to keep speaking. To please them, he preached on until midnight.

One of the young men listening to Paul was called Eutychus. He was sitting on the sill of an open window. Eutychus wanted very much to hear what Paul had to say about heaven and Jesus. Still his head began to nod; his eyes slowly closed. Suddenly he lost his balance and fell out the window! Instantly the Apostle broke off, hearing the boy's shout of horror followed by a dull thump as his body hit the ground.

"My son!" cried a woman's voice from the group. "My son, Eutychus! He was sitting on the window sill! Where is he now?"

"Quickly!" Paul exclaimed, rushing for the door. "Let us see if the boy is all right." Followed by a few men and the boy's mother, Paul clattered down the stairs.

In a few seconds he was at the lad's side. The mother gasped to see her son lying so pale and still on the wet, cold ground.

"He is dead," one of the men declared sadly.

"See, the boy is no longer breathing," another remarked, lifting Eutychus' limp, cold arm. "No one could live after falling from that height."

In grief, the mother began to sob, "Dead? Is it possible? My dear son...."

"Do not be afraid," Paul told her gently as he lifted the young man in his arms and held him to his breast. "He lives! Look!"

Immediately the boy's eyes began to open. Eutychus rubbed his face with his hands and whispered, "Where . . . where am I?"

"My son lives!" the mother cried, joyfully hugging Eutychus as Paul set him on his feet.

"He has risen from the dead!" shouted the other Christians, leaning out the window. "Paul has worked a miracle!"

"O Lord," the humble Paul prayed. "It was You and not I Who worked this miracle!"

18

Final Parting
at Miletus

The next day, as he had planned, Paul left Troas for Jerusalem. On his way to that city he stopped at the seaport of Miletus. The Apostle sent for the priests of Ephesus. When they arrived at Miletus, he addressed them: "I am going to Jerusalem. The Holy Spirit has warned me that I will have to suffer much in that city. But such is the will of God. I accept His will gladly. What makes me weep is the thought that you may fall into sin. Other preachers will come and lie to you. They will try to lead you from the true faith! Remember my warning, I beg you! Recall how I preached Christ to you, day and night, for three years. . . . Now I must leave you . . . and I fear I will never see your faces again. But I put you all in God's hands."

How sad the other priests felt! Their dear father was leaving them forever! Some of the men had tears in their eyes. Even Paul, strong as he was, had to brush the tears from his own eyes. "Let us pray," he said bravely. "God will give us strength to bear every sorrow for His sake."

After they had prayed, the men sadly followed Paul to the dock. Each of them shook his hand long and hard for the last time. . . . Then he boarded the ship. Slowly the boat moved out of the port. With a lump in his throat, Paul watched the men's faces fade away into the distance.

The ship stopped at Caesarea, a seaport not far from Jerusalem. There Paul stayed with Philip the Evangelist. One day a stranger knocked at Philip's door. He introduced himself as the prophet Agabus. The minute he saw Paul, he went right up to him. To the surprise of Paul and Philip, the prophet took Paul's belt and wrapped it around his own hands and feet. "The man whose belt this is will be tied like this at Jerusalem," the prophet warned in a deep voice. Then throwing off Paul's belt, Agabus walked out of the house without another word. Philip and his family were amazed and shaken.

"Paul," Philip's wife began, "must you go to Jerusalem?"

"Stay with us awhile, Paul," Philip begged. "Wait until things calm down at Jerusalem."

"What do you mean by talking like this and breaking my heart?" Paul cried. "It is the will of God! I am ready to suffer all things for the Name of my Lord Jesus Christ!"

19

Captured at Jerusalem

The Christians of Jerusalem gave Paul a hearty welcome when he arrived there. James and many of the other priests came to visit him at Mnason's house, where Paul was staying. James and his companions rejoiced to hear of the many converts Paul had made. For about a week Paul freely preached to the Christians of Jerusalem. Everything seemed to be peaceful. . . .

Then, one day as he was praying in the great Temple, his old enemies spotted him! "Help!" they cried, rushing over and seizing him. "Help! Here is the one who breaks our religious laws by bringing pagans into the Temple!" The men dragged Paul out of the Temple and kept shouting for help. Within seconds a mob had gathered around Paul and the men.

"I did nothing to you!" Paul declared loudly, trying to free himself. "Let me go!"

"Kill him! Kill him!" roared the man who had first grasped Paul's arm.

Immediately the wild crowd took up the cry, "Kill him! Hang him!"

The crowd made so much noise that the Tribune, the chief of the Roman army in Jerusalem, heard it. Looking out of a window of the Tower of Antonia, he noticed a great mob in front of the Temple. Snatching his spear, he sharply ordered several soldiers to follow him: "Quickly men! Trouble in front of the Temple!"

By this time Paul was covered with bloody wounds. His clothes hung in scraps from his body. Crazy with rage, one of the men rushed up to him and dropped a noose over his head. Paul was only minutes away from death. Just then several rough Roman soldiers burst through the crowd. They pulled his enemies away from him and pushed the crowd back. Then they bound him with two heavy, black chains.

"What is the trouble?" demanded the Tribune angrily to Paul. "What did you do to cause this?" Immediately loud cries burst from the crowd:

"Kill him! Kill him!"

"He is a traitor!"

"He ought to die!"

Seeing that all the disorder had started up again, the tribune ordered his soldiers to take Paul to the Tower of Antonia.

"Wait!" Paul cried to the Tribune, "I must ask you something!"

"Do you speak Greek?" the Tribune demanded. "Are you the one who stirred up so much trouble in Egypt not long ago–the one who led four thousand murderers out into the desert?"

"No," returned Paul. "I am a Hebrew from Tarsus. And I beg you, permit me to speak to these people."

"All right," the Tribune agreed sharply, "but make it short!"

Covered with blood and dirt, Paul stood on the temple steps to speak. He motioned with his hand and the crowd became quiet. He then spoke to them in Hebrew: "My Brothers, listen to what I have to say. I am a Hebrew like you. I was born in Tarsus. As a boy, I studied under Gamaliel." And he went on to tell the story of his persecution of the Christians and his conversion on the road to Damascus. So far the people quietly listened to to him. Then he explained, "In the Temple, the Lord appeared to me and told me, 'Go and preach My Name to the pagan nations of the world!'"

The minute Paul said "pagan nations" the mob burst out again in all its wild fury. The word "pagan" reminded the Hebrews again of why they were trying to kill him. They felt he had broken one of their most important religious laws.

"Kill him! Kill him!" angry voices screamed. "Away with him! It is not right that such a one should live!"

The Tribune did not know Hebrew, so he had not understood Paul's speech. However, he could see that it was something Paul had said which had stirred up the crowd's anger. "Take the prisoner to the fortress and whip him!" he ordered sharply. "Then he will tell us what he did to cause all this trouble!" The soldiers immediately seized Paul. But he refused to become frightened.

"Is it permitted for you to whip a Roman citizen without a trial?" he calmly asked the soldier next to him.

In amazement, the soldier let go of Paul and rushed over to the Tribune. "Sir, do you know that the prisoner is a Roman citizen?" he burst out.

"A Roman citizen!" exclaimed the Tribune, shocked by the news. By Roman Law no ruler could punish a Roman citizen without a trial. "You are a Roman citizen?" the Tribune fearfully asked Paul.

"Yes," Paul answered, "I am."

"I paid a very high price to become a Roman citizen," the Tribune said.

"And I," Paul returned, "was born one!"

After the Tribune ordered the soldiers to set Paul free, he turned to the crowd and said, "Call your high priests together. Tomorrow this man will speak before them. Then we shall see if he is guilty or not."

The next day Paul stood before the high priests and other Hebrews in the Temple. The

Tribune and some of his soldiers were also present. "My Brothers," he began, "I have acted with a right conscience in the eyes of God."

"Hit him in the mouth!" shouted the chief high priest.

"Wretch!" Paul burst out in anger. "God will punish you! You sit there to try me for breaking the Hebrew Law. And you break the Hebrew Law yourself by ordering me to be hit!"

Someone from the crowd cried, "How dare you talk that way to the high priest?"

"Excuse me," Paul replied calmly. "I did not know you were the high priest." The high priest said nothing in return. He knew that Paul was right in saying that it was against Hebrew Law to hit a man in the mouth. In fact, for his many evil deeds, he would one day be punished by God. He was choked to death by murderers.

So Paul continued speaking. Then the priests began to argue among themselves over Paul's words. In a few minutes the argument flamed up into a wild fight. Fearing that Paul would be torn to pieces, the Tribune ordered his soldiers to take him away to the Tower of Antonia.

Alone in a room of the Tower, Paul felt

sad and lonely for the first time. But Jesus appeared to His Apostle and comforted him: "Be brave. You have defended My Name well in Jerusalem. Defend it well in Rome also."

Meanwhile the Hebrews' hatred for Paul still burned. About forty of them went to the high priests and said, "Tell the Tribune you wish to hear Paul speak again. Explain that you want to look into his case more carefully. We are going to lie in wait for him along the road to the Temple. Before he gets there, we will kill him! In fact, we have all made a vow not to eat or drink until Paul is dead!"

Paul's nephew overheard these wicked plans. Immediately he raced to the Tower of Antonia and got permission to see Paul. As soon as he entered Paul's room, he told his uncle of the evil plot. Paul then called one of the soldiers and said, "Take this boy to the Tribune. He has something to say to him."

Upon seeing the Tribune, the boy explained the Hebrews' plan: "There are more than forty of them, ready to kill Paul; they are only waiting for you to send him to the Temple.

"You are a very brave boy to tell me," the Tribune told Paul's nephew. "Do not tell anyone else anything about this and leave the rest to me."

That night the Tribune sent Paul to the governor, Felix, at Caesarea. Two hundred soldiers, seventy horsemen, and two hundred spearmen went with him in case the Hebrews should attack him. One of the soldiers carried a letter from the Tribune explaining Paul's case to Felix.

When Paul arrived at Caesarea, the soldier delivered the letter to Felix. Later, the Apostle went before the governor who told him, "I have read this letter from the Tribune. He told me all about you. You are to wait in prison until the high priests come to Caesarea. Then I will hear what each side has to say and judge the case."

Five days later, the chief high priest with a lawyer and some of the other high priests came to Felix's palace. The governor listened to their words about Paul and then told him to defend himself. The Apostle proved himself innocent. So Felix sent all the Hebrews back to Jerusalem. He should have set Paul free, but he was a greedy man. He hoped Paul would pay him money in order to go free. Paul, being poor, had no money so he had to stay in prison.

Even though Felix was selfish and evil, he fell under the spell of Paul's charm. Very often he would send for him and ask him to talk: "I

121

enjoy hearing about the Christian religion. Tell me more about it."

Happy to preach about Christ, Paul told the governor many wonderful things about Jesus. "It takes great courage to follow Jesus," the Apostle declared. "A good Christian must give up all his selfish desires."

Felix did not like the idea of making sacrifices. "Your religion is beautiful, but it is too hard," Felix complained.

"No sacrifice is too hard," Paul returned gently, "if you do it for the love of God!"

❋   ❋   ❋

Felix kept Paul in prison for two years. Then the Emperor Nero called Felix to Rome and sent another governor, Procius Festus, to Caesarea.

After staying in Caesarea for three days, Festus visited Jerusalem. Paul's enemies speedily went to the new governor and asked that Paul be sent to Jerusalem for trial. "This matter is very important. Paul must be tried at once!" they insisted. However, they really planned to kill Paul as he rode from Caesarea to Jerusalem.

But Festus refused to do as they asked.

The governor, Felix, listened to Paul with deep
interest.

"If you want him to be tried, come to Caesarea. Present your case against Paul to me."

Therefore the high priests went to Caesarea and presented to the governor and his council many false charges against Paul. Paul listened very calmly, then defended himself. "You know very well I have done nothing against the Hebrew Law, against the Temple, or against Caesar.

"Do you wish to be tried by the high priests in Jerusalem?" Festus asked him.

"If I have committed a crime worthy of death, I do not refuse to die," Paul answered. "But the high priests can prove none of their false charges against me. Therefore they have no right to try me. *I appeal to Caesar!*"

"Very well, since you have appealed to Caesar, to Caesar you shall go!" announced Festus.

Caesar was the emperor of the Roman Empire. At this time he was Nero. He lived in the great city of Rome in Italy. Every Roman citizen accused of a crime had the right to appeal to Caesar. This meant that the citizen could go to Rome to defend himself before the emperor. Since Paul had appealed to Caesar, Festus had no choice but to send him to Rome.

St. Paul's Fourth Missionary Journey

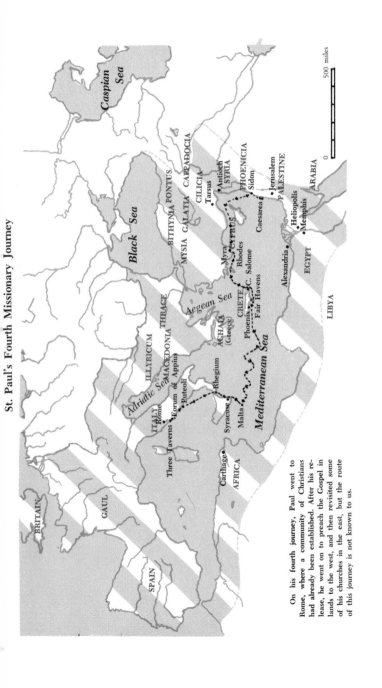

On his fourth journey, Paul went to Rome, where a community of Christians had already been established. After his release, he went on to preach the Gospel in lands to the west, and then revisited some of his churches in the east, but the route of this journey is not known to us.

20

Storm at Sea

Paul and the other prisoners headed for Rome were placed in the care of a soldier named Julius. The doctor, Luke, and Aristarchus, another close friend of Paul's, sailed to Rome with the Apostle. Julius was a very kind man. He let Paul talk often with his friends. When the ship reached the port of Myra in Lycia, all those headed for Italy changed ships.

The winds were against the boat, so sailing was slow and dangerous. The ship finally dropped anchor at Fair Havens, a port on the island of Crete. The captain planned to spend the winter in Fair Havens, but the harbor was not good enough. Therefore, he decided to risk sailing for Phoenis, where the harbor was better.

As the ship began the dangerous trip, a light south wind sprang up. All the sailors were pleased. This meant fine sailing.

Suddenly a wild wind called "Euroaquilo" blew up. This wind was so strong that the ship could not face it. The sailors quickly lowered the mainsail so that the ship would not be tipped over by the raging winds. Looks of fear came across the faces of the sailors and passengers. Would they make it safely to Rome?

To lighten the ship, the men threw over part of the cargo of wheat and the ship's gear. Still the boat tossed heavily in the stormy waters. Great black waves washed over the deck. All were sure they were headed for a watery grave. Paul, alone was not afraid. He trusted God. "O Lord," he prayed, "save us from this wild storm. I put my faith in Your mercy and in Your almighty power."

That night an angel of the Lord appeared to Paul and said, "Do not be afraid, Paul; you must stand before Caesar. And behold, God will save you and all who are with you."

The next morning Paul told the other men of the angel's words. "So, men, be of good cheer," he urged. "I am sure that God will not fail us."

Some of the sailors doubted Paul's words, however. After two weeks of rough sailing, they were thoroughly afraid. At midnight on the fourteenth day, several of them tried to escape in the lifeboat. Paul heard the noise they were making. Going to Julius, he warned, "Unless these men stay on the ship, you will not be saved." Quickly Julius ordered his soldiers to set the lifeboat adrift.

At dawn, Paul, like a father, encouraged the sailors and passengers to eat. "This is the fourteenth day that you all have refused to eat. Because of your fear, you are losing your strength. So let us have a hearty meal before we throw the rest of the cargo of food overboard." Then Paul prayed and broke bread with them.

When the sun had risen a little higher, the men noticed a bay with a beach not far away. The captain decided to risk running the ship ashore. The sailors untied the rudder fastenings, put up the foresail, and headed for the beach.

Suddenly with a loud cracking noise the ship ran aground! The front of the ship was stuck fast in the sea bottom. And the storming waves smashed up the back of the ship. The soldiers drew their swords to kill the prisoners. They did not want any of them to escape.

"Stop!" Julius cried, because he did not want Paul to be killed. "All those who can swim—jump overboard and save yourselves! The rest of us will float in on boards or whatever we find!" Within minutes the foaming waters were dotted with heads moving toward shore. Floating after them were many wet, cold forms clinging to pieces of the ship's deck or mast.

Finally they were safely on the island. Julius counted the dripping, shaking men standing around him. Two hundred and seventy-six men had been on the ship. And all were here before him! Paul had been right! They were all saved!

Hearing the men's shouts and knowing the wildness of the storm, the people of the island ran to the beach. Quickly they built a huge fire so the travelers could warm and dry themselves.

Paul helped to gather wood. As he was throwing sticks into the flames, a snake crawled from the middle of the bundle of sticks. The

The coast of Malta looked grim and desolate as the shipwrecked men struggled toward the shore, clinging to pieces of wreckage.

Paul shook the snake off his hand and it fell into the flames.

little black creature sank his sharp teeth into Paul's hand. "Look!" gasped one of the islanders. "That man must be a murderer! He has escaped the sea, but Justice will not let him live!"

All expected Paul to swell up immediately and die. But the Apostle calmly shook the snake off his hand into the fire. There were not even tooth marks in his skin from the snake's bite. The people of the island, seeing no harm come to Paul, whispered to each other, "He must be a god! Anyone else would be dead from such a bite!"

When he heard of the arrival of the strangers, the ruler of the island went to the beach himself. "Welcome to Malta!" he greeted the travelers as they stood around the fire. "I and my people will be glad to give you food and clothing until you are able to begin your travels again."

The ruler heard the story about the snake and then met Paul. He warmly invited him and his companions and Julius, too, to his house. When Paul learned that the ruler's father was very sick, he asked to see him. Laying his rough, brown hand on the father's old, gray head he prayed to God to cure him. To the whole family's joy and amazement, the sick man sat up in bed. He was completely cured! The ruler could not thank his strange and wonderful guest enough. Soon all the sick of the island came to Paul and were cured.

After a three month's stay at Malta, the sailors and passengers sailed for Italy on another ship. Paul as usual, had preached the Gospel to whoever would listen. He left behind him on Malta many converts. He waved good-bye to these new Christians as he stepped aboard the ship. He felt very sad to leave them. "But the will of God comes first," he told himself as the hills of Malta slipped out of sight. "Now to Rome—to defend Christ's Name before Caesar!"

21

To Rome
in Chains

At Puteoli, a city in Italy, Paul, Luke and Aristarchus left the ship and met some of their Christian brothers. With Julius' permission, Paul stayed at Puteoli for a week. Then with Julius, Paul and his two companions set out for Rome.

At the Market of Appius—forty-three miles from Rome—several Christians met Paul. "It is a great grace to see you, Paul!" one of them exclaimed. "We have heard all about you from some of your converts who visited Rome."

"I have often wished to hear you speak about Jesus," another young Christian added.

"Blessed be God!" returned Paul gratefully. "He has given me the grace to see you and to put my feet on the soil of Italy at last!"

After leaving the Market of Appius, the travelers met another group of Christians at Three Taverns, thirty-three miles from Rome. Many of the Christians knew Paul from the letters he had written to them. They looked upon him as a friend and a father. "We are honored to have you with us, Paul!" they cried, each one warmly shaking the Apostle's hand.

"May the peace of the Lord be with you all!" exclaimed Paul.

Finally the travelers neared the great capital! As the bright white statues and rich marble palaces of Rome met Paul's eyes, his heart leaped. A thrill ran through him. So this was Rome—the greatest city in the world! Little did Paul know that this kingly city would someday be the capital of Christ's kingdom on earth!

For a moment sadness came over Paul. His hands were still chained. . . . But the courageous Apostle lifted his heart to hope. To himself he declared fiercely, "The Word of God can never be chained!"

At Rome, Julius found that Paul could not be tried immediately. So he gave Paul into the care of another soldier. From the Roman authorities Paul also received permission to live with the Christians. However, the soldier who was watching over him had to live with him.

From Paul's right wrist hung the heavy black chain. The other end of the chain hung from the soldier's left arm. Paul's kindness and gentleness toward the soldier softened his heart. He began to listen carefully as Paul spoke of Christ to the other Christians. One day he hinted to the Apostle of his coming conversion, "You have become my father in Christ."

"Yes, my son," returned Paul smiling. "This chain joins not only our hands, but also our hearts!"

However, in all his troubles Paul never thought of himself. There was still so much work to be done for Christ! Many people came to see him. They learned from his words and example how to love God generously. The Apostle also wrote many letters to the converts he had made on his missionary journeys.

Paul wore faded and patched clothes. His skin was rough and sunburned. His beard was thin and his hair was gray. He was not a handsome sight. But people loved him when they came to know him because he had a great heart.

22

A Hero Forever

Very soon the Philippians heard that Paul was a prisoner in Rome. They sent to him one of their priests, named Epaphroditus. "Beloved father!" he cried joyfully when he met Paul. "The Christians of Philippi send you their greetings!" Then the priest went on to tell Paul how worried the Philippians were about him. "We pray for you everyday," he declared.

"Blessed be the Lord Who has sent you to me!" Paul replied gratefully. "The Church at Philippi is my joy and my crown!"

137

One day, among the many people who visited Paul, there was a certain Onesimus. This young man was the slave of a rich Christian named Philemon. He had stolen a large sum of money from his master. Then, in fear, he had fled to Rome to escape punishment. Paul learned of Onesimus' crime from some other Christians.

Little by little he won the young man's heart. Soon he had converted the unhappy slave into a fervent Christian. Then he looked for a way to send Onesimus back to his master. "It is best for you to go back to the house of Philemon," he told the slave. "If you are ever caught by the authorities here in Rome, they will kill you without mercy."

"But Paul, I am so afraid of my master. . . . He will be so angry with me. . . ." Onesimus returned fearfully.

"Now, now, be in peace," Paul comforted him. "I have written a letter to Philemon and explained everything. Listen. 'To Philemon, my dear friend. I send to you my son, Onesimus. Receive him as you would receive my heart. May you welcome him, not as a slave, but as a brother in Christ!' "

Paul was one of the few people whom Onesimus trusted. Believing in his words, the fearful slave went back to his master. Another Christian, named Tychicus, went with him and carried Paul's letter to Philemon.

Because of Paul's words, Philemon gladly forgave Onesimus for what he had done. And several years later Onesimus became a very fervent priest!

* * *

After two years of waiting and working (he even preached to the ladies of Nero's court!), Paul was tried by the Roman court and was found innocent.

Freed from his chains, he went to Spain to preach. He was no longer young, but his heart still burned with love for God. He still wanted to bring many souls to Christ! After visiting Spain, and some other countries, Paul journeyed to Rome once again.

At this time, Nero still ruled the Roman empire. At first he had governed the empire well. Then jealousy and pride had begun to fill his heart. He listened to bad advice. Soon he became cruel and rough. He cared only for himself and for his own pleasure. One night he gave his soldiers secret orders to set Rome

Paul carried on his mission of preaching the Gospel in spite of his chains. "I may be bound," he said, "but the word of God is not bound."

on fire. His plan was to build a new and more beautiful city in memory of himself.

Within a few hours, the entire city was in flames. Word got around that the Emperor was responsible for the fire. A screaming mob, now without homes or belongings, gathered around Nero's palace. "Murderer!" "Criminal!" the angry people roared.

The Emperor shook with fear. He ordered his men to tell the crowds that the Christians had set the fires. With those words, he started the first persecution against the Christians of Rome.

His soldiers were commanded to arrest the Christian men and women, nail them to crosses, burn them alive or throw them to lions. In his great cruelty, Nero thought of all sorts of terrible ways to kill the Christians. One night he ordered his soldiers to tie a group of them to stakes in his private gardens. Then the soldiers covered the Christians with sulphur and tar and set them on fire. Their burning bodies provided light for Nero's evening entertainment. . . .

But Nero died a terrible death. After the persecution, he went insane and was driven from Rome by his many enemies. Full of terror, he fled into the country, but was unable to escape his enemies. So he plunged a knife into his throat and ended his evil life at the age of thirty-two years!

❊ ❊ ❊

Meanwhile Nero's persecution of the Christians was raging full force. Soon Nero's men arrested Paul and many of his friends. Paul was thrown into the Mamertine prison. Shortly afterwards the Roman court sentenced him to die for being a Christian.

Paul listened to the death sentence calmly. He was not afraid. Even though he was old, poor, ragged, in chains, his love for God was strong enough to overcome it all. His heart rejoiced as he thought, "I have fought the good fight; I have finished the course, I have kept the faith. Now there awaits me the crown of glory which the Lord, the just Judge, will give to me."

Paul was sent back to the Mamertine prison to await his execution day. Up to the last minute, the Apostle preached Christ. He even converted his jailers!

On the day of his execution, the guards led Paul forth from the prison. With great courage and joy he walked his last mile to the place of his death. He thought only of heaven. Very soon he would be united forever to his beloved Lord Jesus Christ!

Paul was led outside the city to the place of his execution.

When they reached the spot, the soldiers stripped Paul and whipped him. Then they blindfolded him. Paul knelt to receive the deathstroke. The sword flashed high in the morning sun. Then down it came upon Paul's neck.

His bloody body was carried away by a few faithful friends and buried at the estate of a rich convert, where today stands the majestic Basilica of St. Paul. But his pure soul flew to heaven to join his Divine Master. Now and forever Paul is with his God, for Whose love he bravely and generously walked so many weary miles, preached to countless souls and suffered all kinds of trials—from stoning to shipwreck.

Truly he is a great hero of Christ! For any young boy or girl who is generous, active, ever ready to help others, Paul is the perfect patron. Each one of you can be an apostle—can give Jesus to the world—as he did. Like him, the great Apostle, you can bring Christ into your home, school and community with kind words, happy smiles, good example, and helpful acts.

Daughters of St. Paul

IN MASSACHUSETTS
    50 St. Paul's Avenue, Boston, Ma. 02130
    172 Tremont Street, Boston, Ma. 02111
IN NEW YORK
    78 Fort Place, Staten Island, N.Y. 10301
    625 East 187th Street, Bronx, N.Y. 10458
    525 Main Street, Buffalo, N.Y. 14203
IN NEW JERSEY
    84 Washington Street, Bloomfield, N.J. 07003
IN CONNECTICUT
    202 Fairfield Avenue, Bridgeport, Ct. 06603
IN OHIO
    2105 Ontario St. (at Prospect Ave.), Cleveland, Oh. 44115
    25 E. Eighth Street, Cincinnati, Oh. 45202
IN PENNSYLVANIA
        1719 Chestnut St., Philadelphia, Pa. 19103
IN FLORIDA
    2700 Biscayne Blvd., Miami, Fl. 33137
IN LOUISIANA
    4403 Veterans Memorial Blvd.,
        Metairie, La. 70002
    86 Bolton Avenue, Alexandria, La. 71301
IN MISSOURI
    1001 Pine St. (at North 10th), St. Louis, Mo. 63101
IN TEXAS
    114 East Main Plaza, San Antonio, Tx. 78205
IN CALIFORNIA
    1570 Fifth Avenue, San Diego, Ca. 92101
    278 17th Street, Oakland, Ca. 94612
    46 Geary Street, San Francisco, Ca. 94108
IN HAWAII
    1184 Bishop St., Honolulu, Hi. 96813
IN ALASKA
    5th Ave. and H. St.
    Anchorage, Ak. 99501
IN CANADA
    3022 Dufferin Street, Toronto 395, Ontario, Canada
IN ENGLAND
    57, Kensington Church Street, London W. 8, England
IN AUSTRALIA
    58, Abbotsford Rd., Homebush, N.S.W., Sydney 2140,
        Australia